Kyrie Irving: The Inspiring Story of One of Basketball's Most Versatile Point Guards

An Unauthorized Biography

By: Clayton Geoffreys

Table of Contents

Foreword

There are few point guards in the NBA that can captivate an audience quite like Kyrie Irving. With an incredible ability to score the basketball along with impressive ball handling skills, Kyrie is the epitome of the modern-era point guard of the NBA. His passing skills are rival to few others in the league, making him one of the best point guards in the league alongside Stephen Curry. Kyrie wasn't always this great of a basketball player though. His journey in picking up the game of basketball is an inspiring one in that it's a testament that with hard work comes great rewards. Now playing alongside LeBron James and Kevin Love, Kyrie and the Cleveland Cavaliers are positioned to remain a threat in the Eastern Conference for years to come. Thank you for downloading *Kyrie Irving: The Inspiring Story of One of Basketball's Most Versatile Point Guards*. In this unauthorized biography, we will learn Kyrie's incredible life story and impact on the game of basketball. Hope you enjoy and if you do, please do not forget to leave a review! Also, check out my website at claytongeoffreys.com to join my exclusive list where I let you know about my latest books and give you goodies!

Cheers,

Clayton Geoffreys

Visit me at www.claytongeoffreys.com

Introduction

In their early twenties, most young adults have just graduated college and are looking for jobs, but Kyrie Irving has yet to turn 24 and is already an accomplished multiple-time NBA All-Star, the recipient of the 2012 Rookie of the Year Award, and the 2014 NBA All-Star MVP. Not only that, but Kyrie has been to the NBA Finals at a very young age while most NBA players retire without even having a chance at an NBA championship. However, he would tell you these accolades are par for the course. As he was told by his father, "Stay hungry and humble." This proverb is what continues to drive Kyrie's relentless work on and off the court. In a league that is being dominated by a tide of extremely talented point guards, there is no choice for aspiring athletes but to be great. For Kyrie, his buttery-smooth ball handling, along with his knack for acrobatic finishes around the rim, make him stand out from his contemporaries.

Irving's game is crafty and elegant. He keeps opponents guessing from the top of the key right down to the bucket. His masterful dribbling ability and his superb ambidexterity allows him to keep defenses on their heels. While the 24-second shot clock is ticking, Irving's collection of moves seems to be endless. He zigzags like a chess master. He keeps defenders on their heels and in anticipation of the inevitable and unavoidable show that Irving's hands could do. In one interview, he says:

I just practiced simple moves first—like crossovers, between the legs, behind the back—and then I would work on combinations in isolated situations by myself. Then I would have counters to every move, always being prepared for that—not only that second move, but that third, fourth, fifth move, just in case.

For Irving, each frame of basketball action is a meditation. His mind flips through different scenarios like a statistician running business simulations, and it only takes him a split second to pick a counter-dribble.

Counters that have been built through many years of training with coaches and his father are Irving's bread and butter. His dribbles and his ability to handle the ball both seem like second nature to him and he could very well do them with his eyes closed or even when he's asleep. As Irving was never the fastest nor the most athletic of NBA players, his handles have brought him to places no other point guard has been to before.

Irving frequently reminds the media that he is not just a basketball player. His famous advertising campaign with Pepsi, wherein he dressed up as an old man to challenge young players at local ballparks, garnered millions of views, and earned him the nickname "Uncle Drew," but it is not his first acting gig. Before his NBA fame, he participated in extracurricular drama classes and learned to play musical instruments. He was well liked by his peers not because of his status as a player, but because of the kind of person he was. YouTube interviews with classmates and old teammates show us that Kyrie is someone who just wants to have fun with his friends. And his nature and fun-loving attitude seems evident by the way he plays the game of basketball.

He might be outgoing but, like many of the NBA's talented young men, he is also grounded. Players like Damian Lillard, Stephen Curry, Derrick Rose, Isaiah Thomas, and many more show us the importance of avoiding getting too high or too low. This is not a trend, but rather a skill. This is the attitude they have absorbed through the ups and downs of becoming high-caliber athletes. Parents and mentors may do well to encourage this mentality among gifted players. This was certainly the case with Irving.

Prior to the arrival of LeBron James and Kevin Love, Irving had been the centerpiece in efforts to rebuild the Cleveland Cavaliers. Right out of the draft, 19-year-old Irving established himself as a talented starter through the consistent numbers he put up, averaging 18.5 points and nearly 6 assists a game. He went on to become the best newcomer and the most productive first-year player that year to win the coveted Rookie of the Year award.

Unfortunately, despite Irving's accomplishments, the Cavaliers have not been able to build a winning culture. Some have raised questions about Irving's ability to be a leader as well as a basketball player. He is frequently compared to other point guards who have been able to raise the status of their franchise, like John Wall, Derrick Rose, Russell Westbrook, Chris Paul, and Kyle Lowry. But Cleveland, at that time, was in the process of rebuilding a once great and feared franchise under LeBron. As good as Kyrie Irving is, the Cavaliers were too young and inexperienced to give the star point guard the success he sorely needed to belong to the upper echelons of the NBA.

With the arrival of LeBron James and Kevin Love, a chance arose for Kyrie's name to be cleared and for him to be given recognition amongst the most talented players in the world. The Cavaliers have entered a new era; with high expectations that have brought the franchise to an appearance in the NBA Finals. Although they lost to the eventual champions the Golden State Warriors, Kyrie Irving and the Cavs went into the 2015-16 season with renewed hunger for success. Today, the Cleveland Cavaliers are the best team in the Eastern Conference and they have achieved that with Kyrie Irving nursing an injury during the first three months of the season.

Despite the setback in the 2015 NBA Finals, Kyrie and his super team have had the same kind of expectations to win the title ever since the Cleveland star trio joined forces in mid-2014. The high expectations of winning a championship tend to wear down a franchise, especially on teams that have not had the pleasure of hoisting that lovely golden trophy. From the players to the coaching staff, everyone gets scrutinized. But nobody gets as much scrutiny for failures as star players and head coaches do. Being a star player, Kyrie has had his share of scrutiny for his failure to match expectations as he had to keep away from the basketball court after Game 1 of the NBA Finals due to injury. The Cavs would have been a dynasty in the making had they won that title in 2015.

Other teams have tried to match these expectations and failed. Take a look at the flop of the 2013 talent-heavy Lakers. Scrutinizing famous figures has become even easier with the internet, and so the players' every loss or downfall becomes a sensation, damaging the opinions of sports organizations. However, seasoned teams like the San Antonio Spurs and other Western Conference members have managed to build well-rounded dynasties the right way. Building a dynasty takes time and requires a focus on building up a team, not as just a collection of great players, but as a cohesive entity. From management, to the athletes, to the trainers, to the fans, everyone must bring their "A" game. Staying afloat despite this new wave of scrutiny is just one of the challenges that Irving and the Cavaliers must contend with.

These kinds of obstacles are not new for Irving, and he was scrutinized especially closely during the growing pains of the pre-James years. However, his flashy but effective style of play has quieted his naysayers and established him as one of the elite point guards of the NBA, as confirmed by his many accolades and the many broken ankles he has caused. Still, can he help usher in a championship dynasty for the Cleveland Cavaliers? Judging by his history of transcending his own abilities, his leadership will take the team into a new era, especially playing alongside fellow All-Stars.

Chapter 1: Childhood and Early Life

Fans may think of him as a pure American talent, but Kyrie Irving was born in Melbourne, Australia in 1992. His father, Drederick Irving, was a professional basketball player on an extended stay there, and therefore it was the birthplace of both Kyrie and his older sister Asia. Kyrie's mother was the late Elizabeth, who died when her son was merely four years old. Eventually the family would move back to the United States of America and settle in New Jersey when Kyrie was at the tender age of only two years old.

His father, whose passion for the game was contagious, cultivated Kyrie Irving's love of basketball. Basketball was a routine part of Irving's childhood and youth. As an infant, Drederick would take Kyrie to his pro-am games, and put him on teams with his peers as early as elementary school. With the footage to prove it, Drederick knew that Kyrie had fallen in love with the game of basketball when he was as young as 13 months old. The footage would show Kyrie dribbling a small basketball while looking at his father. He was in only fourth grade when he envisioned his lofty goal: "Play in the NBA." Kyrie's father laid out all the steps that Kyrie needed to take in order to get to the NBA. As all fathers should, Drederick wanted his son to be a much better person and ball player than he ever was. When his son was in eighth grade, Drederick predicted that Kyrie would be the best basketball player in New Jersey. His words could not have been any truer.

While most NBA stars' fathers tend to be absent from their families, Kyrie Irving's father was near perfect in how much he wanted to help his son fulfill his potential and his dreams of being in the NBA. Drederick knew his son wanted this, but also knew from his own experience that it was not going to be easy. However, he saw a bright future for Kyrie because of the boy's unbelievable desire to prove himself. Since Drederick had himself treaded the path of a professional athlete, he knew it was going to be a serious commitment, with hours and hours spent in the gym and on the court. Wisely, he laid out a meticulous plan for Kyrie to follow. There were a few reasons for this diligent planning. Firstly, it was Drederick's own shortcomings that prevented him from playing in the NBA, and he was determined not to let this happen to his son. Secondly, the passing of Kyrie's mother from a sudden onset of sepsis left them both with a gap to fill. Finally, it was his own life experiences that taught him the importance of hard work and dedication.

Drederick Irving's childhood was certainly less than perfect. After his father abandoned the family, his mother raised him and his five siblings in the projects. She kept two jobs and obtained welfare to support her children. These are the life experiences Drederick took to heart. His job as a financial broker on Wall Street taught him about how vicious the competition could be, and he knew his son would need more than a goal written on a sheet of paper. He would need firm direction. He needed a father like Drederick, who was committed to being the best dad he could be, and whose professional basketball career brought many years of experience to the table. Without Drederick Irving's contributions, Kyrie Irving would not be the NBA All-Star he is today. Drederick wanted his son to be able to avoid the pains and the hardships he himself had experienced in his life. The plan was centered on basketball because that was what he and his son loved to do the most.

There is no perfect basketball player, but Drederick Irving made sure he was pushing Kyrie to be as nearly perfect as he could be. He believed in Kyrie's potential to work hard, even referring to Kyrie's motivational drive as a "Bentley's engine," but of course his training was not without its challenges. Kyrie's innate approach to the game was timid; he didn't believe in himself like his father did. Drederick did not see in his son the type-A mentality of the most successful Wall Street workers. From Drederick's perspective, this was an obstacle that would require hours upon hours of practice to overcome. He envisioned his son developing the kind of confidence that comes from knowing you have worked too hard to fail. With Drederick as his coach, in both character development and basketball skills, they ran drills that included dribbling tennis balls, handling basketballs wrapped in a plastic bag, and dribbling at various speeds and with multiple balls. Practicing Mikan Drills was one of the key factors in Irving's smooth finishing ability at the rim. Drederick's other teachings were responsible for Kyrie's well-documented ball-handling ability. As a father, he strived to keep him grounded and to sharpen his competitive spirit. He repeatedly reminded Kyrie that while he was sleeping, someone on the West Coast was putting in work. After many years of development, Drederick felt like his son was able to compete at a higher level, and so he enrolled Kyrie in the New Jersey AAU Roadrunner's program, and the private Montclair Kimberley Academy.

For his part, Kyrie Irving has always recognized the presence and impact of his father on his basketball career. Aside from being his pseudo-coach, Drederick was also Kyrie's standard in terms of how good he wanted to be. He would always measure himself to see how tall he was and how near he was to his father's 6'4" frame. Kyrie always told Drederick that he wanted to become taller and bigger than his father, aside from being a much better player. However, Kyrie would never outgrow his father but would become everything else that he and Drederick dreamed of becoming.

Chapter 2: High School Years

MKA Days

Irving's high school basketball career started at Montclair Kimberly Academy, known also by its initials (MKA). As a freshman standing 5'8" with a frail and skinny body, he averaged 16 points per game, and was awarded the County Freshman of the Year Award. However, compared to the widely-publicized high school phenoms of the past, he was a late bloomer. It did not help that his high school squad was only slightly over the .500 mark. It would not be until his later high school years that Irving became a nationally recruited athlete.

He made his first step toward recognition during his sophomore year. With the help of his trainer, Sandy Pyonin, his abilities improved and he put up a dominating 26.5 points per game, helping MKA win its very first Prep B State title. In some of his more notable games, he scored approximately 47 points.

Seth Bynum, an MKA teammate, recalled Kyrie excelling at every facet of the game. He said, "He was going to go by you if you got on top of him. If you backed away, he was going to hit a three in your face... He was the perfect player." It would seem that, as early as his high school days, Kyrie Irving has had the knack of handling the basketball and putting points on the board.

Off the court, coaches and friends often took note of Irving's humility. Tony Jones, Irving's coach at MKA, praised his grounded attitude.

> Not all the time do you get really, really good people who have an opportunity to achieve their dreams. Ky is so down to earth. Sometimes kids who have the kind of success he's had at his age have this kind of prima donna attitude. He has none of that. He's about as down-to-earth as you can be.

As Irving's game progressed, a more competitive stage became necessary. MKA did not seem like the proper breeding ground for such a talented player as he was. Moreover, the competition he faced while being with Montclair was not up to the challenge of making him a better basketball player. Like many high school talents, he transferred to one of New Jersey's most highly acclaimed basketball prep schools: St. Patrick's. There, Irving faced tougher competition and a better training program that both helped develop his basketball abilities to peak form.

St. Patrick Days

At St. Patrick's High School, Irving really grew as a player. St. Patrick's was always a high school powerhouse in basketball, not only within the state but also on the national stage. The school has produced a lot of NBA players, including Derrick Caracter, Sam Dalembert, and Al Harrington. Under the leadership of Coach Kevin Boyle, the team, which included Irving and current Charlotte Bobcat forward Michael Kidd Gilchrist, won its third consecutive state title. As a junior, Kyrie averaged 17 points and 6 assists per game.

Kyrie Irving was so good in his first season with St. Patrick's that former NBA coach Kevin Boyle went on to say that Kyrie Irving was the best player in New Jersey that year after seeing the kid playing against St. Benedict. An assistant coach with the team also said that Kyrie had one of the best work ethics he had seen in his life. Irving was already training in the gym as early as 6:45 am, even when formal practices started after 7 in the morning. Because of Kyrie's work ethic and his transcendental skills, Boyle has recently said that Irving is arguably the best New Jersey native to ever play in the NBA. Those are serious words considering that Rick Barry, an NBA legend, also came from New Jersey.[i]

As his senior year began, Irving had already established himself as one of the best players in America, and media outlets rated him in their top five or ten. He was highly recruited by a lot of college programs and was arguably the hottest high school prospect in America that year. Irving had plenty of college options, and many notable programs sought Irving's talents. After all, he was a smart investment. His abilities could help bolster a school's championship pedigree, and his status could improve the reputation of the school especially because he was thought to be an immediate NBA prospect. Irving, however, had his goals as a student as well as a player, and he wanted to choose a program that would take advantage of his game and his brain. He eventually narrowed down his choices to Duke, Seton Hall, Texas A&M, Georgia Tech, and Kentucky. On October 22nd, 2009, he publicly declared that Duke was his college of choice, in part because of its established camaraderie. Moreover, Duke was under the leadership of legendary college coach and successful Team USA head coach Mike Krzyzewski.

College programs are a gateway to the pros, and going "one and done" is not uncommon, making the challenge of building a long-term competitive team a difficult one. However, Duke possessed the X-factor that Irving was looking for, and he was impressed with the way everyone from top to bottom made a contribution. The coaches built strong relationships and understood the game of basketball deeply. In an interview with Duke's basketball media team he said: "What separates Duke from other schools is just love and trust and the brotherhood that came before me." Duke was also one of the winningest college basketball programs in the United States. With Duke, Kyrie not only had the chance of developing and learning from the best coaches but could also become an NCAA champion.

After making his decision, he set his sights right back on his final year as a high school player. His commitment to Duke seemed to only strengthen his dedication on the court. As a senior, he continued to mature as a player, leading St. Patrick's to a 24-3 record. With Irving pitching in 24.7 points per game, the team finished in first place at the Union County Tournament. However, because of out-of-season practices, St. Patrick's was banned from participating in the state tournament. Despite this, Irving's future looked bright. As a top recruit, he would have the opportunity to participate in the widely publicized high school events, such as the McDonald's All-American and the Jordan Brand Classic, where he was a co-MVP with another future NBA prospect, Harrison Barnes. He was also a member of the Junior National Select Team in 2010 and was a gold medal winner with Team USA in the FIBA Under-18 Tournament. All the labor in the gym, practicing dribbling with his left hand, and all the drills he ran with his father were finally paying off. Another item on his NBA to-do list had been checked off. Going into college, Kyrie was ranked as high as number two among high school prospects and was the best point guard in the high school ranks. He was on his way to Duke to further hone his talents and to take a step closer to the NBA.

Chapter 3: Training with Pyonin

Irving seemed to make an effort to keep the right kind of mentors around him. Sandy Pyonin (pronounced pie-YO-nin) played a pivotal role in developing Irving's basketball skills during his formative years.

People close to Pyonin often bring up the fact that he is so dedicated to basketball and the nurturing of players' work ethic that he does not even own a cell phone. During Irvin's high school years, Pyonin acted as his miyagi-sensei. During the summer, they had workouts six days a week. After full skill training sessions, Pyonin often implemented one of his tough strategies, and would have Irving and his other charges playing full-court games to 100, with each basket counting as only one point.

One of Sandy Pyonin's other alumni, Randy Foye of the Denver Nuggets, said in an interview that Pyonin helped straighten his vision and meet his goals by helping him stay off the streets. In a Sports Illustrated article he says that without Pyonin he was "in danger of becoming another statistic."

Pyonin is a hard-nosed coach and a true basketball connoisseur. He is a gym teacher at a Hebrew day school, Golda Och Academy, and an AAU coach, but these run-of-the-mill titles should not fool you. More than anything, Pyonin is a machine that churns out NBA players. He is like Freddie Roach to Manny Pacquaio, and the Midas of the basketball coaching world. The Wall Street Journal called him a "grassroots legend." His relentless work ethic came from being cut from his basketball tryouts, after spending 10 hours a day putting work into his craft. From then on, Pyonin became a basketball wizard, practicing in his backyard and studying TV games, and brought this dedication to his coaching philosophy. He has trained the likes of Randy Foye, Al Harrington, and Dahntay Jones, and has been one of the key sparks in Irving's life. Pyonin was the funnel that channeled

Irving's work ethic, passion, and his father's life lessons into his becoming a star player for Duke University.

It was Drederick who found out about the New Jersey legend and had him mentor Irving. Their training tales are well-documented and legendary. During the New Jersey summers, rain or shine, Pyonin would pick him up in his trademark minivan. After a quick drive to the local community center, they would go to work. Pyonin was highly committed to Irving's development, and in addition to the 100-point full-court games, he implemented other unorthodox tactics to develop Irving's grit and conditioning. Sometimes, he would put five other kids against Irving. Every summer, Irving's practice time was between five and ten hours a day, six days a week. This long and strenuous training methodology came from his philosophy that a strong mental game is necessary to succeed. In an interview with Blue Devil Nation, Pyonin said: "I try to work with them on the mental aspect of the game as well.

Get them to concentrate on the mental aspect of the game. I'm really big on that, where other... well, most other coaches don't emphasize that enough."

In his NBA Rookie of the Year speech, a humbled and grateful Irving did not forget to thank Pyonin for playing an essential role in the development of his basketball career.

Chapter 4: College Years at Duke

For Duke, the 2010-2011 season looked extremely promising. With the Plumlee brothers, Miles and Mason, and many Duke veterans on board, they were hoping for Irving's strength to lead their team to another NCAA national title. They were optimistic after their previous year, coming off a 35-5 season and winning the National Championship. They were poised to win a second straight title, especially with a much better team coming into the NCAA tournament.

Duke got off to a hot start, and Irving did not fall short of Mike Kryzewski's expectations. In the 11 games he played for Duke, they went 10-1, and he averaged 17.6 points a game. He was scoring at an extremely efficient clip. His field goal percentage was 53%, while shooting 46% from downtown and 90% from the charity stripe. On December 1st, in a game against Michigan State, Irving scored 31 points on an efficient 66% shooting. It was the fourth time in Duke's history when a freshman scored 30 or more points. His 13 of 16 shooting from the free throw line also set records as number one for most free throws scored as a freshman, and tied for first in free throw attempts. During their season opener against Stanford, he recorded 9 assists as a starter, setting a record for most assists as a Duke freshman playing in a season-opening game.

Unfortunately, his record-setting performances would come to an abrupt end. His college career was short-lived, as a toe injury derailed his future at Duke and dampened his chances of staying for multiple years. Despite playing fewer than a dozen college games, Kyrie Irving was obviously much more talented than the rest of his college batch mates. He had learned more than he needed in Duke and was already good enough to take his talents to the big leagues.

On April 6, 2011, after a week of discussion between Irving and his family, it was announced that Irving would forgo his three years at Duke and join the 2011 NBA Draft. Irving felt it was only right that he should enter the NBA, despite the oncoming lockout. His family, friends, and coaches supported the decision unanimously. He was already that good, even though he played only 11 games in college. Kyrie had the tools, the talent, and the potential to make it big in the NBA. However, he promised his father that he would finish his degree while playing basketball in the NBA.

Chapter 5: Kyrie's NBA Career

The Draft

The 2011 NBA Draft was regarded, at the time, as a comparatively weak draft class. With the exception of Kyrie Irving, the media focused its discussions on how many picks in the lottery positions were toss-ups. However, this draft contained a lot of hidden gems, like finals MVP Kawhi Leonard, Chandler Parsons, Kemba Walker, and All-Star Klay Thompson. Kyrie Irving, however, was highly coveted and was the consensus pick for the top overall draftee.

In a league that was becoming full of a generation of All-Star caliber point guards, every franchise wanted a piece of the point guard pie. Because of their role as the floor general and the up-tempo style of play that is common in today's game, they have the most potential impact on the court. A savvy point guard has the ability to command attention and leverage to make his entire team better, and he is currently seen as a fundamental building block for teams looking to contend. For example, as of 2014, the Phoenix Suns have three point guards who can start in Dragic, Thomas, and Bledsoe. Come 2015, the Suns have two starting point guards in Bledsoe and Brandon Knight. The contending Bulls have former MVP Derrick Rose (albeit he is injury prone), the Wizards have John Wall, the Oklahoma City Thunder has the explosive Russell Westbrook, the Portland Trailblazers have Damian Lillard, and the Raptors have Kyle Lowry. Stephen Curry is one of the leading guards representing an elite Golden State Warriors team and has been the best point guard in today's NBA game.

Even in 2011, the point guards representing the 2011 NBA landscape seemed to predict this trend. Every GM in the lottery knew they could have a chance of revamping their franchise with Irving's rare all-around, well-polished game. Whether it was the Toronto Raptors, the Minnesota Timberwolves, the Cavaliers, or any other team fortunate enough to come away with him, it seemed highly likely Irving would end up being the number one pick especially with how unpolished the rest of the draft class was.

Kyrie Irving, even if you put him in different draft classes, was in a level head and shoulders above his peers. At almost 6'3", Kyrie was a comparatively tall point guard and has always had a good NBA-ready body though he was not as strong as other point guards. With his skill set and his ability to run a team, most scouts compared the young Irving to that of established point guards Mike Conley and Chris Paul. But, as we all would see later on in his career, Kyrie became a much different kind of point guard than both Conley and CP3.

Kyrie was often regarded as a "true point guard" in every sense of the word. While most other point guards in today's game look for their own number most often and always put the scoring burden on their shoulders, Irving could run a team with his ability to handle the ball and see the floor. Make no mistake,

Kyrie Irving could score as well as any other player at his position. But what made him different than other scoring point guards was the fact that he looked to facilitate first. Irving was just a player who scored whenever he found an avenue to do so or if his teammates were not in the position to do so. Moreover, what made him a true point man was the fact that Irving has always had the personality of a charismatic leader who could get the team's attention.[ii]

Kyrie Irving could do everything that a point guard could do at an individual level. Irving's handles were always a thing of beauty, no matter what league you look at. His ability to dribble the ball, coming into the NBA Draft, was already miles ahead of his peers and may have even been better than most NBA point guards that time. His sickest move was his crossover dribble, which was reminiscent of the great Allen Iverson. Irving dribbles the ball far outside his shoulder and then crosses it over to the other hand so fast and so well to elude defenders and even have them on their heels or on their backside. When Kyrie is able to avoid the initial defense, he is very good at finishing at the rim with either hand. He was never the most athletic or the strongest player but Irving had the ability to finish with either hand, hang in the air, and contort his body mid-air to finish layups even with the body contact.[iii]

While he could easily get to the basket with his marvelous ball-handling ability, Irving also had a good form on his jump shot, which he could hit off the dribble from anywhere on the floor, including outside the three-point line. Other good penetrators did not have a good jump shot in the early years of their careers. But Kyrie has had that ability at an early stage in his basketball career and it was also a big weapon of his. Because of his shooting, Irving became an efficient player in college with percentages of 50 percent from the floor, 45 percent on three-pointers, and over 90 percent from the free throw stripe. Kyrie Irving's excellent penetrating skills and his ability to shoot the jump shot off the catch or off the dribble made him a terrific one-on-one player and someone very tough to guard because of the many weapons he could utilize.[iv]

Athletically, Kyrie Irving was never the fastest, the strongest, or the highest leaper of point guards. But he had enough athletic ability in him to blow past defenders in a blur. Despite looking frail and skinny, he was deceptively strong and could finish well at the basket with his hang time up. Defensively, Irving was always fast and quick enough to keep in pace with his assignment. He also has quick hands that can get steals easily, especially against slower players. On top of that, Kyrie Irving is big enough to shadow and get physical with smaller point guards and has a considerably long wingspan for a player his size.

The biggest red flag on Kyrie Irving was his health and durability. He only played 11 games in his lone playing year with Duke in college.[v] The NBA has had a long history of players with sky-high potential but who have had troubles with staying healthy. Sam Bowie, who was taken ahead of Michael Jordan in the 1984 NBA Draft, was a very good prospect with a high potential. He had enough talent in him for the Blazers to pick him ahead of Jordan. Sadly, Bowie struggled with injuries early in his career and it ended abruptly. Greg Oden, also picked by the Portland Trailblazers, was chosen as the top pick in 2007 and ahead of Kevin Durant. Oden was a very dominant big man in college on both ends of the court. He had the makings of being the best center in the NBA. Sadly, he also could not get healthy and his career ended early. Lastly, a third Blazer by the name of Brandon Roy developed into an All-Star player in the NBA and was arguably considered in the discussion of best shooting guards in his best years. But he suffered continuous knee injuries that forced him to retire in his mid 20s. No matter how good an NBA prospect may be, his talents could be for naught if he was injury prone. That was what teams feared about Irving.

Kyrie Irving, having played only 11 games in college, also lacked a lot of experience especially in the big league. He was a high school standout in the Jersey area, where basketball is played at a high level. But high school is a different playing field compared to college. And of course, the NBA is at a much tougher level than college. The lack of Irving's experience in college was a big question mark with regard to his capability of playing against elite defenses.

Even though Kyrie Irving had transcendent ball-handling ability and even though he was always a good decision-maker, he also had the tendency of getting too much in love with his dribbles. He would sometimes get into a zone where he would rather put on a show with his dribbles and he would forget about the game and his teammates. At times, that tendency led to turnovers, bad offensive sets, and poor shot selection.[vi] Irving's defense also needed work. He had the tools to become an elite defender. He has the size, the wingspan, and the speed to be able to defend other point guards well. The problem was that his defensive IQ was far below his offensive IQ. He could guard well on the ball but was too inexperienced and immature to guard off the ball. He could get too caught up on playing the passing lanes or getting ready to play offense to the point of losing track of his defensive assignment or getting picked off by screens. Hence, Kyrie Irving was someone whom you could not really rely your all on the defensive end, especially as a youngster.[vii]

Kyrie Irving was, without argument, an inexperienced young player who was also suffering an injury in college. Like all NBA rookies coming out of college as a teenager, Kyrie needed a lot of work, especially on his weaknesses. But he was too good a prospect as an NBA point guard to pass on because of his magical handles and his gifts on the offensive end. Irving was someone you could forgive for not playing his all on the defensive end because he was so good on offense and on running team sets.

On May 17, 2011, the NBA Draft Lottery took place at the Prudential Center in New Jersey. Statistically, the odds were best for the Minnesota Timberwolves, who performed a miserable 17-65 in the previous season. However, in the history of their franchise, they have never had a first pick in the draft, and luck did not seem to be on their side. On top of that, it is well known that the team seated for the best position does not often win, as they are afforded only a 25% chance of winning. Since 1990, there have only been three teams that have won the lottery from the best position possible. The next two on the list were the woeful Cavaliers and Raptors, two teams who had lost their franchise players, respectively LeBron James and Chris Bosh, to the infamous Miami Heat. In years prior, they had some luck in the draft, with the Cavaliers coming away with LeBron James in 2003, and the Raptors winning the 2007 NBA Lottery on a slim 8.8% chance.

The Cavaliers had obtained another pick from a trade with the Clippers, which would be the lucky pick that would bring hope of taking them back to the dominance they experienced with LeBron James. Getting first pick was a miracle, as it came with the pick that had a 2.8% chance of winning the lottery. Their pick, which had the second best chance of winning, landed in the fourth position.

It immediately became clear that Irving would be the chosen one to fill LeBron's shoes. The comparisons between Irving and James were on everyone's lips. People wanted to know if Irving could do what LeBron did. Irving's father would quiet critics in his interview with ESPN reporter Heather Smith:

> Well, I just told Kyrie to be himself. Kyrie and LeBron are two different players. At this particular moment, it is really about Kyrie. No disrespect to LeBron or anything, but I think Kyrie brings a lot to the table. I'm excited for him.

Irving started and ended his draft workout tour in Cleveland. To preserve his value and prevent any injuries, Irving had only one workout for the Cavaliers, training with numerous coaches to raise his value, including Robin Pound, a strength and conditioning coach who specializes in plyometric exercises and exercises involved in the draft combine. Pound, having dealt with pre-draft development for many years, was the expert who could boost Irving's case as the number one pick. Irving was poised to impress scouts, GMs, and coaches, especially with his "intense competitiveness" that Pound noted. Having seen many players come and go, this was a factor that Pound used to measure the longevity of an NBA athlete, and he believed that it was this fire that would carry Irving for years to come.

Irving also maintained a laser-sharp focus in his draft combine workouts. During interviews, his answers showed his state of mind. He deactivated his Twitter account, helping him focus purely on his draft workouts. "I don't have Twitter," he said. "I don't feel the need to have Twitter right now. I'm just focused on getting better."

After draft workouts, it became evident that Irving, with his top-notch skill, would come out on top. He set himself apart in the draft, and became a consensus #1 pick among experts.

On June 23, 2011, the 2011 NBA Draft took place. Draft day was special for Irving, wondering whether he was going to go first or not. He knew he wanted to be in the NBA, he knew he was too good to not make it into the NBA, and he knew he deserved it because he had put in the hours. Between the guidance of his father, the grueling time with Sandy Pyonin, games for Montclair Kimberley Academy and St. Patrick's team, his college career, and his rehabilitation process, June 23 felt like the fruition of all hours he spent working.

As David Stern stood on the podium, Irving could feel the anxiety seeping into his gut, the kind of energy that comes with experiencing a monumental moment as any 19-year-old could encounter. In 2013, an interview with *USA Today* revealed that he wasn't sure whether he was going to go first, but then Stern said, "With the first pick of the 2011 NBA Draft, the Cleveland Cavaliers select Kyrie Irving." He had finally realized a lifelong dream of making it to the NBA, and jubilantly hugged his family members and tightly embraced his father.

This moment was a manifestation of the dream that Kyrie and Drederick Irving had in their minds more than a decade ago. Drederick only dreamed about his son being the best guard in New Jersey. But never did he dream of Kyrie being the best prospect in the 2011 NBA Draft. The goal written by a fourth-grader on a piece of writing paper more than a decade ago had been fulfilled. Neither had made promises to produce one of the best guards in the league, but Irving was about to become a national star and had all the makings in him to make a global impact on the game of basketball.

However, he knew that this was just the beginning of his career. The words "stay hungry and humble" rang in his ears. Many athletes find that the money, fame, and attention make them lose sight of their career at the draft, but Irving knew how far he had come and how far he had left to go. He knew he wanted to become one of the greatest point guards that had ever graced the game of basketball, which is why he set new goals for his rookie year. He recorded a goal for himself that he would average a certain amount of points and assists, and win Rookie of the Year. The "Bentley engine," as his father called him, definitely knew how to drive himself.

As in most drafts, there was speculation about whether Irving was the right pick. *Fox Sports* wrote that Irving was the type of athlete who could "alter the franchise's fortune." The media's doubt only added fuel to the fire that was Irving's rookie year.

Rookie Season

Irving's rookie year had to wait until December to begin because of the 2011 lockout. Many players took this as an opportunity to relax, but Irving kept his goals in mind and worked on his game. With Micah Lancaster, he kept his skills sharp. The lockout finally came to a halt, and Irving had the opportunity to show that he was more NBA-ready than any other members of the 2011 Draft. Whether or not it was deliberate on Irving's part, it was inevitable that the media were going to compare him to LeBron's Cleveland legacy. Statistically, one could compare the two as high school seniors, and see that LeBron was playing on a different level. James had dominated his final high school year, averaging almost 32 points, 10 rebounds, and 5 assists per game. Irving's statistics, 24.7 points, 5 rebounds, and 7 assists, were by no means an easy feat, but it was clear that James was a legend of the kind that comes once in a blue moon. Not to demean James or anything, Kyrie was also a rare talent especially with his wizardry in handling the ball. Though it may have been humbling to receive comparisons to James, Irving would filter out the noise and focus on the Cavaliers.

The only thing the two had in common was the position of their picks. For a player like Irving, who was very good at picking his spots on the floor, he and his father knew comparisons to James would not help his game, and it was this type of focus that helped Irving stay grounded. He knew which circumstances could directly affect him, and worked solely on those. For Irving, this was a 17-65 Cleveland team that was far from its winning days with James and needed time to rebuild. With many of the veterans gone, like Zydrunas Ilgauskas and Mo Williams, it was a brand-new project for Irving. Coming into the 2011-12 NBA season, the Cleveland Cavaliers just came from their worst season since drafting LeBron in 2003. With a 19-63 win-loss record, they needed a lot of room to improve. Luckily, Kyrie Irving was there to help them recover from losing LeBron James in 2010. But Irving had a big load to carry in his rookie season. Other than him, the team's best player was an aging 35-year old Antawn Jamison, who was a former All-Star but was, at that time, far beyond his peak form although he could still play and score at a high level. Other than rebounding center Anderson Varejao and athletic wingman Alonzo Gee, the other players wearing the Cavaliers' uniform were too young, inexperienced, and unskilled to be relied on in tight situations. In his first professional game as an NBA player, Irving scored 6 points against the Toronto Raptors. In January, his numbers picked up as he scored in double figures 16 times and posted a career high of 32 points against the New Jersey Nets. He was awarded Rookie of the Month for his ability to consistently put up strong numbers, and led the team to an 8-12 record by the end of January.

With the inexperience of the Cavs roster and their lack of veteran presence on the scoring end, Kyrie Irving immediately picked up the cudgels as Cleveland's best player that time. Irving dazzled crowds with his awesome ball handles, with his ability to elude defenders, and with his acrobatic hang-time finishes at the basket. Kyrie brought new life to the Quicken Loans arena after a very disappointing previous season. Many people came to watch his ball wizardry on the hard floor. Quickly enough, Kyrie Irving became a crowd pleaser and a Cleveland favorite. Natives of Cleveland were brought new hope with a future budding star in their Cavaliers team.

Kyrie Irving became the uncontested go-to guy of the Cleveland Cavaliers. He was the top scorer and the top facilitator. With his phenomenal pace as a rookie, he was quickly elevated as the favorite to win the Rookie of the Year Award. Even as a newcomer, he did not back down against the top point guards of the NBA and even against the best players of the league. While most star rookies could simply only play ball at a high level, Kyrie Irving could do more than that. He exuded a lot of confidence from his near 6'3" frame. On the floor, he did not play with rookie jitters and felt at home even when playing against elite players. Kyrie moved with such grace, confidence, and enthusiasm that it seemed like he was beyond his playing years. Everyone immediately saw that this kid was a star in the making. They weren't wrong.

In the middle of the season, the leading rookie in the NBA was chosen to play in the 2012 Rising Star Challenge for Team Charles Barkley. Kyrie Irving immediately showed to the world that he was the best young player in the NBA. Even when he was playing alongside and up against sophomore stars, Kyrie looked and felt as if he was the best player on the floor. Even older players gave way to Irving. At the end of the night, Kyrie Irving was indeed the best among rookies and sophomore in the NBA. He scored 34 points along with a perfect 8 of 8 from three-point range. Kyrie won the Rising Star Challenge MVP award. That was the first of what would become a pile of individual awards for Kyrie Irving's career.

In March and April, Irving kept up with his consistent play, and he would win Rookie of the Month again for March. In terms of his individual goals, he met some of his expectations with his consistent play. He achieved his goal of averaging at least 17 points per game, and by winning the Rookie of the Year award.

The 2011-2012 season was a learning experience for Irving. In his first year as a pro, he learned what set the NBA game apart from the college game. Under Byron Scott, he learned how to navigate the pick-and-roll offense and create scoring opportunities for his team. Scott knew the tricks of the trade, having played a key role in the development of Chris Paul when the two were on the New Orleans Hornets squad, and his vast knowledge helped Irving master the ropes of the professional game.

The Cavaliers improved to a 13th-place finish in the Eastern conference. Their record was 21-45, just 4 games behind the 10th place Detroit Pistons. It was a small improvement for the Cavaliers, and showed the value that Irving brought to the team. Combined with his Rookie of the Year award, things seemed to be looking up for the Cavaliers. At the end of the lockout-shortened 2011-12 NBA season, Kyrie Irving averaged 18.5 points, 3.7 rebounds, 5.4 assists, and 1.1 steals in only 30 minutes per game. He also shot about 47 percent from the field, nearly 40% from three-point territory, and 87 percent from the free throw line. His percentages from the floor were all very impressive, considering he was just a rookie player and considering that team defenses were focusing on him because of Cleveland's lack of offensive options. With his outstanding performance as a rookie, Kyrie Irving almost became a unanimous Rookie of the Year winner. He garnered 117 out of a possible 120 first place votes for the best newcomer award. As the league's 2012 Rookie of the Year, Irving also got a unanimous selection to the All-Rookie First team.

Barely coming off his 20th birthday, Kyrie Irving has already made his mark on the NBA in just his first year.

In his Rookie of the Year speech, the people Irving thanked included his father. He appeared serious as the humbled Irving spoke, but did not hesitate to break out in a smile when Kyrie mentioned how they were going to celebrate. Watching his son receive the award, all their conversations and coaching sessions flooded his mind. There could not have been a more proud father.

Second Season, First All-Star Appearance

In Irving's sophomore season, there were not as many changes coming to the Cavaliers roster. But they did, however, upgrade their young core via the NBA Draft. Their poor performance landed them another opportunity in the draft as landed the fourth pick, with which they selected Dion Waiters. He was often compared to Dwyane Wade, and it was hoped that together, Irving and Waiters could make a dominant backcourt. At nearly 6'4", Dion Waiters was a bit undersized for the shooting guard position. But Waiters came into the league with a strong body and a lot of athleticism. As he was often compared to Wade, Waiters had good handles and could get his own shot off the dribble or finish at the basket. He was a mediocre shooter but was good enough for the NBA. The knock on his game, however, was that he needed the ball in his hands to be productive. That meant taking away possessions from Kyrie Irving. The Cavs bench also got an upgrade on big men with rookie Tyler Zeller, who played fantastically in his college years.

Irving gained valuable experience and lessons in the offseason when he played for the Team USA Select Team prior to the start of the next basketball calendar year. Kyrie Irving played phenomenally for the Select Team. He was so good that he earned praises from Team USA main roster after he scored 11 points when the Select Team beat Team USA 14-11 in a short scrimmage during training camp.

Irving's highlight during the Team USA training camp was when he challenged the legendary guard Kobe Bryant to a one-on-one game and even told the Black Mamba that he could beat him. That was an amazing display of confidence on the part of Kyrie Irving, who had just finished his rookie year. He challenged a five-time champion and a then 14-time All-Star to a game. That was something not all 20-year-olds had the guts to do.

It was also a symbolic gesture because Kobe Bryant had also challenged an NBA great to a one-on-one game when he was still in his early 20s. Kobe once challenged and trash-talked the great Michael Jordan multiple times when the Mamba was still a youngster. When Kyrie did it to him, it was a passing of the torch from an NBA legend to an up and coming superstar. Kobe Bryant has since said that Kyrie Irving (and Russell Westbrook) is his favorite player in today's game because of the confidence and skills he exudes.[viii] Those are some high praises coming from a first-ballot basketball hall of famer.

Kyrie, however, would not have the same productive offseason as the Cavs had coming into the 2012-13 season even after gaining priceless experience with Team USA. Irving broke his right hand after slapping his hand on a wall in frustration. He was required to repair it through surgery. That meant that Irving would not be able to work on his game as hard as he would have wanted to in the offseason. The slap on the wall was a bad mistake for such a young player. It was uncalled for, especially since the Cavs needed him to get better before the next season. Nevertheless, everyone needs a couple of learning experiences in their youth. Kyrie was not an exception. It was a learning experience that would remind him to keep his emotions in check in order to avoid unnecessary setbacks to his young career.

The 2012-13 NBA season turned out to be Kyrie Irving's breakout year as an established All-Star. Not to demean his accomplishments as a newcomer the previous year, because he was already a breakout player in his rookie year. But his second year was when he actually was able to fully showcase his wares and his talents to the world by increasing his productivity, all while playing a more defined leadership role for the Cavs on top of his scoring and facilitating duties for the team.

Irving suffered more injuries during the 2012-13 season. But those injuries were minor and only forced him to miss a few games. He broke an index finger early in the season in a game against the Mavs. He also broke his nose following a game against the Milwaukee Bucks. The broken nose required Irving to play with a black protective mask for a few games. That was almost the same black protective mask that Kobe Bryant wore just a few months ago after he broke a bone in his face. While wearing the mask,

Kyrie Irving scored 41 points, which was then his career high, against the Knicks. His 41 points made him the youngest player to score 40 in the world's most famous arena. That goes to show that the confident Irving plays his best especially when he plays in front of the biggest crowds and under the brightest lights.

Despite the Cleveland Cavaliers playing the same dismal brand of basketball they had been playing post-LeBron, Kyrie Irving remained the lone bright spot for the struggling franchise. He increased his productivity game by game and was levels better than he was in his rookie season. His increased production and his crowd-pleasing style of basketball made him a crowd and league favorite. He was so good and so magical as a player that coaches chose him to play as a reserve in the 2013 NBA All-Star game. That marked his first All-Star selection. He was still in his second year but was already an All-Star caliber player. As a 20-year old, Irving joined the likes of Kobe Bryant, Magic

Johnson, and LeBron James as 20-year old All-Stars. Kyrie was once again a participant of the Rising Stars Challenge. This time, he played for Team Shaq.

The 2013 All-Star Weekend was a busy three-day event for Kyrie Irving as he would participate in the event for all three days. First up, he played the same type of showtime basketball he had played the previous year in the 2013 Rising Stars Challenge. The highlight of the night was when he crossed Brandon Knight over for an ankle breaker a basket to the "oohs" and "ahs" of the delightful crowd. The crossover was so quick and so masterful that Knight fell on his backside. That crossover remains in many highlight reels till this day. Next up, Irving participated in the three-point shootout. Not really known as a three-point shooter, Kyrie Irving nonetheless won the event. In the main attraction of the All-Star Weekend, Kyrie scored 15 points and assisted on 4 baskets in his first ever mid-season classic game. It was a good albeit busy

All-Star weekend for a young Kyrie Irving, who was just enjoying his time in the best way he could.

However, Kyrie's All-Star Weekend was the best stretch of his second year because the Cavs remained awful the rest of the season. Despite that, the season marked a leap in Irving's production. Playing a more central role for the Cleveland squad, he averaged 22.5 points, 3.7 rebounds, 1.5 steals, and 5.9 assists per game. He also shot 45 percent from the floor and 39 percent from three-point land. The Cavaliers ended up with a 24-58 record, once again finishing in 13th place. Even with a better lineup than the previous season, Byron Scott had made no visible progress and was therefore fired, bringing about Irving's first coaching change. He was noticeably shocked, and mentioned that "a piece of [him] felt missing" after the departure of the man he referred to as his "basketball father."

Irving has shown a tendency to develop extremely close relationships with the mentor figures in his life, and he has never been shy to show his appreciation for them. It was no different with Byron Scott, who was his first-ever NBA coach. The stoic Scott, with his reputation for developing teams with high-caliber point guards, taught Irving many things, and his previous relationship with Chris Paul and Jason Kidd proved to be a huge benefit to Irving. However, now he was gone, which was so painful for Irving that it was speculated that he might move to the Lakers when they hired Byron Scott as their new head coach.

Third Season and All-Star MVP

The Cavaliers added good talent to their roster in the offseason of 2013. The Cavs once again struck gold when they were able to get the top overall draft choice of the 2013 NBA Draft. As the 2013 draft class was considerably weaker than the 2012 class, none of the draftees was a favorite for the top overall pick. Nerlens Noel had a strong case as the top overall pick but he was mired with injuries. There were several good point guards and wing players in the draft but the Cavs did not need any more of those. What they needed was a forward who could produce. So they went on to draft Anthony Bennett with the top pick. The pick was controversial, considering that there were more talented players in the draft class.

The beginning of Irving's third season was marked by some bold moves by the Cavaliers. With Irving a year away from contract extension talks, they needed some talent and leadership to match him. After firing Byron Scott, they rehired their old coach, Mike Brown. Brown brought a winning pedigree from his previous stint with the Cavaliers, and it was clear that they were trying to replicate some of the culture they had with LeBron James. This new coach brought an emphasis on defense with the signing of Andrew Bynum, and with the drafting of their new number one pick, Anthony Bennett, the Cavaliers looked like a team in the playoff race in a rather weak Eastern Conference. This was only the second time in league history that a team rehired a fired coach. Mike Brown had been fired back in 2010 in the hopes of making LeBron James stay with the Cavs.

It was not out of the question that the Cavaliers could be contenders this season. They signed Jarrett Jack, who had contributed to the success of the Golden State Warriors as a sixth man and as a mentor for the young Stephen Curry. The Cleveland front office thought that Jack might be able to bring the same kind of production to their bench as he did for Golden State. The Cavaliers' major off-season acquisition was former All-Star and former dominant big man Andrew Bynum, who had rested his knees and was looking to hop back into his Laker form. At his healthiest, he brought a championship reputation to the Lakers, being able to man the paint with his height and wingspan. Just a couple of years before, he was considered to be one of the NBA's more dominant centers and was considered a rival of Dwight Howard. Between the dominant frontcourt of Bynum and Varejao and the improved Dion Waiters, this could be the season that they could redeem themselves from their 2010 off-season blunder of losing LeBron James. If things jelled the way the Cavaliers' organization hoped, Irving might finally have a winning record to back up his accolades and would be recognized for his ability to lead the team. However, the 2013-2014 campaign was mired with injuries, harmful speculation, and an inability to win.

The season started off poorly for the Cleveland Cavaliers. Despite their poor record, Irving played with his characteristic grounded mentality. In November, Irving cleaned the stat sheet with 20.6 points and 6 assists per game. He tied his career high from his previous season, scoring 41 points in a face-off against John Wall and his Washington Wizards. However, that would be their last win for the month as they went on a 5-game losing streak. It did not seem like Irving's results translated well for the team, as they chalked up a 4-12 record by November 29.

The Cavs' 2013-14 season was once again a one-man show starring Kyrie Irving. None of his teammates performed and produced well enough to get the team into playoff contention. Andrew Bynum struggled to remain healthy once again. Dion Waiters, although scoring at a good pace, was inefficient and inconsistent. He also struggled playing off the ball as Irving was the main ball handler for the Cavs. Varejao, who was a rebounding demon the previous season, was also struggling to get back to the form he had prior to ending the 2012-13 season with an injury.

Most glaring of Cleveland's entire roster problems, Anthony Bennett failed to live up to the hype as the top overall draft pick. Bennett was quickly being considered as a big draft bust because he was unable to produce right away. He was undersized as a power forward but was too slow as a small forward. Hence, Cleveland struggled to find a place for him in the lineup. And, to put it bluntly, he was just awful in his rookie season. Anthony Bennett averaged only 4.2

points and 3 rebounds while shooting a very poor 35.6 percent from the floor in only 12 minutes per game. Perhaps the Cavs made a poor choice in drafting Anthony Bennett. Or perhaps Bennett was just swamped by the hype of being the top pick of the draft.

With the trade deadline nearing and with the Cavs still far from playoff contention, the front office made a midseason change in the roster. Andrew Bynum only played in a total of 24 games for the Cavaliers, and additionally, was a distraction. His misconduct halted practices, leading to eventual suspensions. Then came rumors that he wanted to leave the Cavaliers and, whether they were true or not, they contributed to the organization viewing the Cavaliers as home to a losing culture. The Cleveland Cavaliers traded Andrew Bynum away to the Chicago Bulls in exchange for veteran forward and former All-Star Luol Deng. Deng would fill up the small forward hole that the Cavs had had ever since LeBron left the team. Bynum was a big gamble for the team because he was simply dominant when at full health. Unfortunately, he could not stay healthy and had problems with being lazy. Luckily, the Bulls were willing enough to take him in and to trade Deng. In some ways, Bynum was still able to help the Cavs because Deng could bring tough perimeter defense and a veteran presence for the team.

For Irving's part, he still remained the same spectacular showtime player he always was. He carried the Cleveland load on offense and tried to make the team relevant as much as he could. However, he would fail in that regard but was still one of the top point guards in the league. As the All-Star Weekend came about, Irving started for the first time in his career. Kyrie Irving became one of the youngest All-Star starters and he did so in only his third year. As a third-year player, Irving was already a two-time All-Star. He made his mark by dominating with 34 points and 14 assists. Irving almost singlehandedly brought back the East Team when the Western All-Stars were threatening to run way with the win. Irving's clutch performance in the fourth quarter of the midseason classic earned him the honor of All-Star MVP.

His fame skyrocketed because of his social media campaigns as well as his skills. The Uncle Drew Pepsi campaign significantly increased Irving's popularity. Although it was not a deliberate attempt to earn votes for Irving, there is no doubt that it helped Irving break into the mainstream. Irving also developed into one of the game's biggest clutch players. He went into fourth quarters more ferociously than he did in the first 36 minutes of the game. His ability to play clutch in fourth quarters earned him a second nickname—Mr. Fourth Quarter.

After one of his most memorable moments, Irving still had work to do to help his struggling team, decimated by injuries and a lack of chemistry, break into the playoffs. Anthony Bonnet was out for a total of 19 games, and one of their key pieces, Varejao, would miss about a quarter of the season due to back pain.

There was also frequent speculation about whether Irving got along with Dion Waiters and the coaching staff, which served only as another distraction for the team. Waiters needed the ball in his hands to be effective. And, as a point guard, Kyrie Irving needed the ball more. Hence, there were chemistry issues evident between the two when they were both on the floor.

The team's chemistry issues continued, resulting in a 33-49 season. For the fourth year straight, the Cleveland Cavaliers would be missing out on the post-season, entering the off-season as another lottery team. The inability of the Cavaliers to get into the playoffs under Kyrie Irving's leadership led many people to doubt Irving's ability to make a team into a winner. He was always a fantastic and talented player but Cleveland's losing ways got Irving criticized and scrutinized for his lack of a playoff appearance. But who could blame Kyrie? The Cavaliers were simply struggling to remake the roster after LeBron James left them. Bad draft choices, poor offseason acquisitions, and a couple of different yet unsuccessful coaching staffs had all contributed to why Kyrie could not get into the postseason.

Fourth Season, Enter LeBron and Love

Entering his fourth year, Irving had experienced shifts in his organization's management, played under two coaches, experienced the arrival of two top-four lottery picks who had both underplayed their draft hype, and yet he still managed to achieve an All-Star MVP nomination, a Rookie of the Year award, two All-Star appearances, and the NBA Three-Point Shootout win; and to outstandingly represent Team USA in the FIBA World Cup. Despite lacking a winning record and of course a playoff appearance, his career had been marked by individual accolades. A player can only do so much amidst the chaos of a struggling franchise that has recently made bad choices in free agency and in hiring a coaching staff. The ups and downs of Irving's world would become amplified in one of the most remarkable events in the history of sports.

In his second stint with the Cleveland Cavaliers and with only one season after returning to the Cavs, Mike Brown was once again fired abruptly. The Cleveland front office hired David Blatt, a longtime Euroleague coach. Blatt spent decades in different European nations as both a player and a coach. He also won championships as a coach in Europe and was one of the most decorated head coaches in Euroleague history.

In another unlikely draft lottery, the Cleveland Cavaliers once again won the number one overall draft choice for the 2014 NBA Draft. The Cavs had only a 1.7 percent chance to get the top pick in the draft. That was the third time since 2011 that the Cavs were able to get the top overall draft pick in the lottery despite having low chances of getting the highest draft choice. The 2014 NBA Draft was said to be the deepest draft class in recent years and Cleveland was lucky enough to be able to get the number one pick in such a good class.

The 2014 NBA Draft class was headlined by names such as Andrew Wiggins, Jabari Parker, Joel Embiid, Marcus Smart, and Julius Randle. There was no consensus top draft choice but most scouts believed that the number one draft choice should be either Wiggins or Parker. Wanting a young and athletic wing player to run alongside Kyrie and Waiters, the Cleveland Cavaliers selected Andrew Wiggins. Wiggins was already an established defender in college, a very athletic wing, and a player with a growing offensive repertoire.

In an attempt to propel the team to victory, the Cavaliers organization underwent one of the biggest off-season transformations possible for an NBA team. They were able to get arguably the best rookie for the 2014-15 season as well as a decorated Euroleague coach who brought a lot of defensive toughness alongside an offensive strategy centered on team play in order to manage the young egos of the Cavaliers squad. Irving also signed a 5-year $90 million contract extension. It looked like the team had a young, exciting core consisting of Irving, Waiters, Bennett, and Wiggins.

The Cavaliers were ready to start a slow but steady rebuilding process centered on the young and uber-talented Kyrie Irving and rookie sensation Andrew Wiggins under the leadership of a new head coach who brought a new philosophy to the Cleveland franchise. But the tides turned quickly in favor of the Cleveland Cavaliers. LeBron James suddenly opted out of his one-year player option in his contract with the Miami Heat to test the free agency waters. LeBron had just been in the NBA Finals in a losing effort against the San Antonio Spurs a few months prior to free agency. He was intent on going to a new franchise to win with younger and more talented players or on forcing the Heat to secure more assets for another championship run. Several teams with a lot of salary space were courting LeBron James, including the Los Angeles Lakers, the Dallas Mavericks, and the Cleveland Cavaliers. Everyone remembers how LeBron had spurned the Cavs back in 2010 and went to Miami to form a super team alongside Dwyane Wade and Chris Bosh. With fate weaving its thread, LeBron James chose to go back to the Cleveland Cavaliers. Cleveland's prodigal son was coming home to play alongside Kyrie Irving.

The news that LeBron would go back to Cleveland shook the Cavaliers as much as it did the rest of the league and its fan base. With his sudden re-integration, plans to win titles became immediate. The team would have to look for even more talent to bolster their chances of becoming an Eastern Conference powerhouse. Another talented player, Kevin Love, was also in dire need of going to a winning franchise but was stuck with a big contract in Minnesota. He was looking to get away from the Timberwolves and people began to look at the Cavaliers as a possible destination for the All-Star power forward. Everyone knew that LeBron James was in a "win now" mode and was not in the mood of going through a rebuilding process with the Cavs. While Andrew Wiggins had the potential to become a superstar in the future, he was still raw as a rookie and might not be able to help the King to win a ring as quick as possible. Moreover, he was playing the small forward position and could possibly contend with LeBron for minutes at that spot. Hence, if anyone in the team was going to be traded for Love, everyone thought it would be Andrew Wiggins, who had not even played a single minute for Cleveland.

The team finished their transformation in a surprising but predicted move, trading away their two Canadian number-one draft picks, Anthony Bennett and Andrew Wiggins, for Kevin Love of the Minnesota Timberwolves. Love had something in common with both Irving and James. Like Kyrie, he had never been to the NBA playoffs because the Wolves were in a perpetual rebuilding status in his stint with the team. And like LeBron, Kevin Love had a "win now" mentality. They capped their off-season by adding veteran forward Shawn Marion and LeBron's good friend, Mike Miller. With the influence of LeBron, the Cavs also signed one of the King's favorite teammates, James Jones, for additional floor spacing. The entire dynamic of the team had been shaken to its core, and a new era opened up for the Cavaliers. The team no longer belonged only to Irving. Though Kyrie would remain the team's biggest asset because of his youth and talent, the leadership and alpha reins were turned over to the four-time MVP and two-time NBA champion LeBron James. But James could not win alone and needed both Irving and Love to play at the highest level possible. The three All-Stars ushered in a new sports culture for the city of Cleveland and the Cavs had the biggest chances of getting a top playoff spot to end the franchise's postseason drought that started in 2011.

After a successful gold medal FIBA World Cup campaign and winning MVP honors, Irving brought new growth to the table. Now that he had played with the new generation of American All-Stars, like Rose, Demarcus Cousins, DeMar DeRozan, Curry, Thompson, and Harden, Irving had a taste of what it was like to win at the highest level. He was also a little bit jealous of how some of his peers had been able to get to the playoffs. Winning is contagious and addictive. The gold medal victory only urged Irving to play harder for some gold in the NBA. This was an important experience for Irving, considering the obvious magnitude of the impending season.

The team had a shaky 6-7 start, showing a trend toward changeability in their winning and losing streaks. Winning games against the East's top-tiered teams like the Raptors and the Hawks and taking blowout losses against Detroit and others only added more fuel to their fire. It was also an understandable struggle because the trio of superstars was still adjusting to one another. Kyrie and Love were both used to having the ball in their hands on almost every offensive possession. They were still trying to understand the tendencies of their fellow All-Stars. In the midst of this upheaval, Irving remained his consistent self. His stats were nearly identical to his previous season, maintaining a 20-point per game and 5-point assist average even while he was playing with two other alpha players who scored just as much as he did. It was because Irving saw less defensive pressure focused on him because James and Love were too good to leave open. Despite the media portraying the Cavaliers as a team in chaos, Irving was a professional in his approach, and remained the same crafty player who can create plays. Unfortunately, a quarter into the season, another misfortune befell the Cavaliers: Varejao, their only reliable center, was lost for the remainder of the season.

This was the best team on which Irving had ever played. Despite a record hovering around the .500

mark, Irving's previous Cavalier lineups never made it out of the pits of the Eastern Conference. One of his highlight moments came in their very first home game. Irving was heard over a body mic asking Mike Miller, "Is this similar to what a playoff game feels like?" Hope like this gave Cavaliers fans a reason to be excited, and also gave young fans a chance to relate to him as they experienced the novelty of the playoff-like intensity together. It was also an insight into the mind of Irving. This was the same kind of spark that propelled him as a child to embrace hard work; the same kind of spark that led to all the dribbling drills with tennis balls and basketballs wrapped in plastic bags. Irving had a glimpse of what the limelight could feel like, and it only motivated him to stick to what makes him so good: hours upon hours of focused practice.

From a year-to-year standpoint, the Cavaliers have not met expectations, but the subpar start was great for Irving. Having results too easily has made athletes complacent, as many who won championships early in their NBA career can attest. Three-time champion Dwyane Wade recalled in one interview wondering if the road to his first championship had been too easy. After struggling for several years, Wade understood what it really took to become a champion—exactly the kind of funneled pressure that has molded Irving.

In the middle of the season, the Cavaliers needed to shake things up in order to bolster their claim as a top Eastern Conference contender. Dion Waiters, who was often lost on offense after the arrival of James and Love, was part of a three-team trade that sent JR Smith and Iman Shumpert of the New York Knicks to the Cavs, along with 7'1" Nuggets center Timofey Mozgov. While both Smith and Shumpert provided good production at the wing position, it was Mozgov whom the Cavs really coveted in that trade because they were in dire need of a center after losing Varejao to injury. Timofey was not the best back-to-the-basket center but he was always good at finding an open position under the basket for easy dunks. Thus, he became an ideal player, especially with the paint open because Irving and James sucking out the defense.

For Irving's part, having LeBron James and Kevin Love helped him a lot, especially in alleviating defensive pressure. In Irving's first three years with the Cavs, he had no other teammate that could score just as much as he could. Therefore, opposing teams would focus their defensive strategy on stopping Kyrie Irving. But with James and Love, teams could not double Irving and sag off the two All-Star forwards because both LeBron and Kevin could score in bunches as well. The big duo allowed Irving to play isolation more often and also allowed him to get open three-point looks outside the perimeter.

Irving's terrific and consistent play earned him a third straight All-Star game selection. He and LeBron James became the first Cavaliers duo to be selected to the All-Star game since Mo Williams and LeBron had done it several years back. Kyrie played 19 minutes in the All-Star game and was able to score 11 points, which was far below his MVP-winning performance a season back.

Kyrie Irving was also the owner of two of the highest scoring totals in the 2014-15 NBA season. He scored 55 points against the Portland Trailblazers on January 28. He made 11 three-point baskets—one shy of tying the record held by Kobe Bryant. His 55 points was the highest total ever scored in the Quicken Loans Arena and the second highest that a Cavaliers player has ever scored. Barely two months later in March, Irving re-established a new career high of 57 points against the then defending champions, the San Antonio Spurs. The Spurs could do nothing to stop Irving who just scored at will. including a three-point basket to send the game into overtime. The Cavs won the game in the extra period. With his 57 points, Kyrie Irving broke the franchise record for most points scored in a regular season game. The previous record was 56 by teammate LeBron James, who held the record for 10 years.

At the end of the regular season, Irving was near his usual numbers. He averaged 21.7 points, 3.2 rebounds, 5.2 assists, and 1.5 steals per game while shooting 46.8 percent from the floor and a career high of 41.5 percent from beyond the arc. He helped the Cavs power through the rest of the season after an early struggle. Kyrie's efforts earned him his first ever All-NBA team selection as a member of the Third Team. Cleveland earned the second seed in the East with a 53-29 regular season win-loss record. With the postseason berth on hand, Kyrie Irving (and Kevin Love) was headed to his first-ever playoff appearance.

Irving, together with LeBron and Love, was set to face the Boston Celtics in his the first-round series. In the first-ever playoff game in his very young NBA career, Kyrie Irving scored a game-high 30 points for the Cavs. The Celtics were able to put up a good fight in the first quarter but the Cavaliers' defense suddenly turned up a notch in the next three quarters to limit Boston for the rest of the game and to win it 113-100.

The Cavs Big Three each led the team in the three main statistical categories. Irving led in scoring, Love led in rebounding with 12 boards, and LeBron James assisted on 7 baskets.

In Game 2, the Cavaliers found it even more difficult to get rid of the Celtics. Boston was even grittier than before and they just would not let the Cavs win the second game so easily. It fell on LeBron James to take over the fourth quarter just to keep the Boston Celtics at bay. LeBron scored 15 of his 30 points in the final quarter to win the game 99-91, improving the series lead to 2-0. In his second playoff game, Kyrie Irving scored 26 points in another good game for the playoff rookie.

When the series moved to Boston for Games 3 and 4, the Cavaliers were thinking of taking it one game at a time. They had all the tools to sweep the Celtics out of the playoffs but they focused on the game at hand. Had the Cavs been too excited for the second round, the Celtics could have given them a run for their money because the Celts played Cleveland almost even in Game 3, except for a good opening quarter for the Cavaliers. LeBron scored 31 for a total of 61 over the last two games. He also collected 11 rebounds. Meanwhile, Kyrie Irving dialed down his productivity to just 13 points in Game 3. Irving shot only 3 out of 11 but was able to dish out 6 dimes to win the game by 8.

Kyrie Irving, with the help of LeBron James, was finally able to get to the second round by defeating the Celtics in Boston. Kyrie scored 24 points while LBJ chipped in with 27. Despite sweeping the C's, the journey to the second round was not at all very easy. The Cavs may have won four straight games but it was only Game 1 that they won decisively. The Celtics played a very physical brand of basketball that made it difficult for Cleveland to get into their offense easily. Boston was so physical that Kevin Love was not saved from any harm. Love got tangled with Kelly Olynyk early in the first half when they both went for a loose ball. Olynyk got his right arm hooked with Kevin's left as they both tried to get possession. As Kelly Olynyk went down, he brought Kevin down with him. The entanglement dislocated Love's left shoulder and forced him to leave the game in pain. The injury would sideline Kevin Love for the rest of the postseason. It was an unfortunate incident for a man who was in his first playoff series and for a team looking to go as deep as they could in the postseason.

The Cavs had to go on without the third head of their three-headed monster. It fell upon Irving and James to pick up Love's scoring and on backup big man Tristan Thompson to get the rebounds that Love would have gotten. Nevertheless, Cleveland was still mighty strong as a unit even without Kevin Love. They were still the toughest beasts of the East. And they needed all that toughness as they were going to face the physical defense of the Chicago Bulls in the second round.

The Cleveland Cavaliers suffered their first loss of the postseason in Game 1 at the hands of the Bulls. It seemed like the Cavs were too rested and rusty after ending the first round a lot early than most other teams. On the other hand, the Bulls ran roughshod over Cleveland in the first quarter as they ended the opening 12 minutes with a 15-point lead. Chicago held on to the lead they built despite the runs attempted by the Cavs to win the game 99-92. It was a battle of elite point guards as Kyrie Irving, in a losing effort, scored 30 points versus the 25 of former MVP Derrick Rose.

In Game 2, the Cavaliers flipped the pages on the Bulls. It was Chicago that looked rusty in the second game of the series as the Cavs held a 20-point lead at the end of the first quarter. It was a lead built high enough because the Bulls never came close. LeBron James lorded over the Bulls' defense with 33 points. Meanwhile, Kyrie Irving played one of the most efficient ball games he has ever played. He scored 21 points on only 9 shots. He made most of his contributions from the free throw line.

Game 3 in Chicago had the most dramatic of finishes, no matter from what perspective you look at it. The Cavs played the Bulls even and toe-to-toe right down to the final second of the ball game. It was a typical story of one-upmanship as neither team would give room to the other. When the game was tied at 96 and down to the final seconds, Derrick Rose and the Bulls had possession. Rose dribbled to the top of the key and rose over Kyrie Irving's outstretched arms to hit a banking three-point shot right as the buzzer sounded. It was a tough loss for the Cavs, who suffered a bad game from their star point guard. Kyrie; he scored only 11 points on 3 of 13 shooting, although he played good defense on Rose on that final possession but the former MVP was just able to see enough room for that banker. LeBron scored 27 for the Cavs in the losing effort. The Cavs found themselves down 1-2 in the series.

If you thought Game 3 was dramatic, Game 4 was just as good. The game mirrored the previous one. Neither team gave the other any room to breathe and they were trading punch after punch. But the final punch belonged to LeBron James. When the Bulls were up 84 to 83 in the dying seconds, David Blatt called timeout for the Cavs, who had possession of the ball. Blatt drew a play that would have LeBron inbounding the ball to most probably their best clutch player Kyrie Irving. But LeBron told Blatt to change the play and to give him the final shot. It's a good thing David Blatt listened to his four-time MVP. LeBron caught the inbound pass at the left corner and rose up to shoot a three-pointer that went down the net smoothly. Just like that, it was game over and the Cavs won the tough one, 86-84. The shot was just two days after Derrick Rose hit his banker. Indeed, the series was a game of "What you can do, I can do as well."

With both Kyrie, who only scored 12 points on 2 of 12 from the field in Game 4, and LeBron shooting poorly in the last two games, the All-Star duo were due for their respective slumps to end. And there was no better way to end their shooting slumps than to do it in the same game. As seen from the last two outings, the Bulls played the Cavs tight in all four quarters. Game 5 was no different. It was another tight one that would have gone to the wire had Jimmy Butler hit a three-point basket to send the game to overtime. But Butler missed it and the Cavs won 106-101. LeBron James was the top scorer with 38 big points and 12 rebounds while shooting 14 out 24. Meanwhile, Kyrie also broke out of the slump with 25 points on 9 out 16 from the floor. Cleveland went up 3-2 in the series and was one game away from getting to the Conference finals.

The series was played as tight as ever and neither team won a game decisively over the other except for the Game 2 victory by the Cavs. With Game 6 played in Chicago, you might normally expect another wire-to-wire ball game. And you'd be correct to expect that. However, it was only true in the first quarter. The Cavs played the Bulls tight in a high-scoring first quarter that ended 33-31. But that 31-point first quarter was all the Bulls could muster up for the rest of the game as the Cavs clamped down on defense. The Bulls could only score 42 over the next three quarters and the Cavs were finally able to dispatch them with a 94-73 victory. It was an all-around effort and backup point guard Matthew Dellavedova came out as the unlikely hero by scoring 19 off the bench. Though the Cavs would proceed to the next round, they suffered another end-of-the-round injury. Kyrie Irving had to leave the game early in the second quarter after he landed awkwardly on Tristan Thompson's foot. He would not return and scored 6 points in only 12 minutes. The Cavs were hoping that their All-Star point guard would not suffer the same fate as Kevin Love.

The Cavaliers saw themselves back in the Conference Finals for the first time since they lost to the Orland Magic in 2009. They were going to fight for an NBA Finals spot against the top-seeded Atlanta Hawks, who had the second best record in the NBA in the regular season. The Hawks had also beaten the Cavs three out of the four times they met in the regular season.

Atlanta was a force to be reckoned with, especially with how well they moved the ball around, as the Spurs always have. They also had four All-Stars in the team with Al Horford, Paul Milsap, Jeff Teague, and Kyle Korver. The only knock on the Hawks' game was that they played team ball so well that they had no superstar to go to whenever the game was tight.

For the Cavs, Kylie Irving was available to play in the Conference Finals but was severely limited. It was a bummer for the Cavs because they needed everybody to play their best as the Hawks had home court advantage. It turned out that not having home court advantage was never really a bother for Cleveland. LeBron and JR Smith off the bench exploded for the Cavs to steal Game 1, 97-89. Though the Hawks started the game well, the Cavs won every other quarter after the first to ultimately win the opening game. Still nursing his injury, Kyrie played only 27 minutes and scored only 10 points.

When the Cavs led by only 5 points at half time and with Kyrie sitting out Game 2, LeBron James led a third quarter charge that extended the Cleveland lead to 18 entering the fourth quarter. The Hawks defense would allow the Cavs only 10 points in the whole fourth quarter but they themselves could not score enough to trim the lead down to a manageable deficit. Hence, the Cavs won the game, 94-82 despite having only one All-Star playing. James systematically destroyed the Hawks by scoring 30 points, collecting 9 rebounds, and dishing out 11 assists for a near triple-double performance. By winning the first two games, the Cavs not only stole home court advantage, but also stole two of the possible four home games away from Atlanta.

In Cleveland, the Hawks played the Cavs toe-to-toe for the whole 48 minutes of the game in the hope of regaining the home games they lost to Cleveland. Kyrie also rested for the second straight game. With Irving resting, LeBron had to pick up everything the team gave up to rest their All-Star guard. Luckily, LBJ was up to the task. He gave everything he could to win the game in overtime and to get the team a 3-0 lead over the series. With the Cavs down by two in the final 36 seconds of overtime, LeBron hit a three even after favoring his leg. A possession later, James hit a floater to seal the 114-111 win for Cleveland. At the end of the exhausting overtime game, LeBron James had a stat line that could shame even Oscar Robertson himself. LBJ scored 37 points, rebounded 18 misses, and assisted on 13 baskets for a fantastic triple-double performance despite being basically a one-man team versus the Hawks' four All-Stars. Though the Hawks were a very good team, this was the time that they needed a superstar who could shine under the spotlight in tough situations. Unfortunately, they did not have one and were one loss away from exiting the playoffs. People expected the Hawks to at least fight off the Cavs in Game 4 to try to extend the game and make it hard for the Cavs to reach the NBA Finals.

Unfortunately, they had all but given up on fighting. As soon as the ball was tipped, the Cavs scored at will against the Hawks. On the other hand, Atlanta seemed drained of energy and did not seem desperate to keep their season alive. With Kyrie Irving back in the lineup, the Cavs had all the tools to decisively win the game and the series. Irving scored 16 points in only 22 minutes of action while James had 23 on another near triple-double performance for the Cavs team that won the game by 30 points.

For the first time since 2007, the Cleveland Cavaliers were going to the NBA Finals and had another chance at winning a title for Cleveland. For LeBron, it was his fifth straight NBA Finals appearance, beginning from his Miami days in the 2011 Finals. It was his sixth Finals appearance and his second for the Cleveland Cavaliers. On the part of Kyrie Irving, it was the first season in which he made it into the playoffs and he did not expect that, in his first playoff season, he would make it as far as the Finals. It was a childhood dream coming true for the kid out of New Jersey, who only dreamed of being an NBA player but never an NBA champion.

The Cavaliers were going to have to fight a grueling series against the best regular season team, the Golden State Warriors, who had won 67 games out of a possible 82. The Warriors were coming off their best regular season and were on pace to make history by winning an NBA title for only the second time in franchise history. 2015 NBA Most Valuable Player Stephen Curry led Golden State, alongside Klay Thompson, Draymond Green, and Andre Iguodala, among other excellent role players. It was a dream match-up of the two best ball handlers in the world. Kyrie Irving had been considered the best ball handler in the NBA ever since his rookie year. He could cross anyone over and elude defenders with his in-and-out dribble or his behind-the-pack crosses. But Curry was also a much improved ball wizard in his 2015 MVP season. He didn't have the same quick and elusive crossover that Irving had, but he was just as ambidextrous in handling the ball and had the ability to dribble with finesse and grace to trick and avoid defenders. But Curry's best weapon was always his deadly three-point shooting. It was a shot he could put up from anywhere within 30 feet away from the basket, from any situation, and from any dribble.

As expected, Irving and Curry dueled in the Bay Area as soon as Game 1 of the NBA Finals started. The Cavs started the game better than the Warriors but Golden State slowly chipped the 10-point lead away for a wire-to-wire fourth quarter. In the Warriors' final play of the fourth quarter, with the game tied at 98 apiece, they went to the MVP Steph Curry. Curry went up against Irving. When Steph was able to lose Kyrie with his dribble, he went straight to the basket for what seemed like an uncontested go-ahead layup. But Irving suddenly rose up from the floor behind Curry and cleanly blocked Steph's layup attempt. It was a game-saving block of a shot that would have given the

Warriors the lead. LeBron missed his attempt at a game-winner and the game went into overtime. Unfortunately, overtime was cruel to the Cavs. Cleveland struggled to score in the entire extra five minutes. Adding insult to injury, Kyrie Irving aggravated his left knee injury and limped off the court in the overtime period. He would never return. James could only score 2 points for the Cavs in overtime and Cleveland could not steal Game 1 from the Warriors. Irving had 23 points and Curry had 26 for the elite point guards' one and only Finals matchup. LeBron James was the star of the game in a losing effort. He had 44 points but failed to deliver in overtime.

With the injury he suffered in Game 1 of the Finals, Kyrie Irving was forced to be sidelined the entire Finals series. He had to undergo surgery for the injured knee while the Cavs went on to win Games 2 and 3 to lead the series 2-1. But with a lineup change that involved Andre Iguodala starting for the Warriors, Golden State won the next three games of the series to win their first NBA title since 1975. For Irving, had he been healthy along with Kevin Love, many people speculated that the Cavs would have won the championship. But staying healthy is part of the game and that was where the Cavs failed. But it was not a bad first playoff appearance for the fourth-year player Kyrie Irving, who would unfortunately miss all basketball activities until late November of 2015 because of the injury he suffered in the Finals.

2015-16 Season

Irving missed the first one and a half month for the Cavaliers because he was still recovering from his knee surgery. He returned to practices in late November but only made his season debut on December 20. He has since played limited minutes for the Cavaliers team that was staying on top of the Eastern Conference despite Kyrie's absence. The team core stayed the same but the Cavs added veteran Richard Jefferson to spell LeBron at the wing position and also signed former Cavalier All-Star and scoring point guard Mo Williams to take care of the point position in Irving's absence. Varejao returned from injury and he played behind Timofey Mozgov at the center position to give the Cavs a deep frontline especially with Love back healthy and with Tristan Thompson coming back to the roster with a huge contract.

Kyrie Irving has only played limited minutes since his return from injury and has appeared only five games. In the five games that he has played, Irving averaged 13 points and 3.4 assists in barely 22 minutes of action. He has shot an awful 34 percent from the floor while still trying to find the proper rhythm as he was absent from the basketball floor since the NBA Finals. Kyrie was one of the leading vote getter among backcourt players in the first returns of All-Star votes even though he has played only a handful of games. That is a testament to how popular and well known a player Kyrie Irving is. He beat out other East point guards who have performed better than him throughout the season, such as Kyle Lowry, Jeff Teague, and Reggie Jackson. If the fans voting for Irving as a starter in the All-Star game keep up the pace until the final ballot returns, Kyrie is set for his fourth straight All-Star game appearance and his third straight start in the midseason classic.

Chapter 6: International Play

Kyrie Irving was already a part of the Team USA program soon after winning the Rookie of the Year Award in 2012. It was in the Team USA training camp where he famously challenged Kobe Bryant to a one-on-one game and even told the legendary Laker that he could beat him. His confidence and his bravado in confronting the five-time champion made Kobe Bryant admire him so much. Kobe even ranks Irving atop the list of his favorite young players in today's NBA game. Though he failed to make the main roster then, he was sure to be a part of future Team USA lineups.

Before the 2014-2015 season, Irving represented Team USA in the FIBA World Cup. It proved to be a vital summer for Irving, as it was also a reunion with his former college coach, Mike Kryzewski, who was the head coach of the USA program.

For Irving, making the cut was not going to be easy. The competition for the guard position was fierce, and included talented guards like Stephen Curry, Klay Thompson, Derrick Rose, and Damian Lillard. Eventually, the cuts were announced, and Irving had earned a spot on the team. He would be sharing the role with Derrick Rose and Stephen Curry, after Damian Lillard and John Wall got cut. For the coaches and the managing director Jerry Colangelo, creating a gold-winning roster was a difficult process. Colangelo said, "Since taking over the USA Basketball Men's National Team program in 2005, this was without a doubt the most difficult process we've gone through."

The road to the gold started off in the group stages, where Team USA achieved a clean sweep of 5-0, beating Finland, Turkey, Ukraine, New Zealand, and the Dominican Republic. Irving's ability to take advantage of Kryzewski's floor spacing system allowed him to thrive in the open court. It also allowed him to play one-on-one easily since he was rarely doubled with all the superstar talent in the Team USA roster. The international style of play took advantage of his skill in fast break situations.

Team USA dominated the entire tournament, and ended up taking home the gold. In a convincing 129-92 victory over Serbia, Irving showed the world that he could compete with the best. His play in the gold medal game, including 22 points, earned him the title of Most Outstanding Player at a young age of only 22 years old.

Irving took this experience home with him in the form of a renewed sense of purpose. The elite competition brings out the competitive spirit in all of Team USA's players especially on the very confident point guard Kyrie Irving who plays his best under the bright lights, in front of the biggest crowds, and on the biggest stages.

Chapter 7: Irving's Personal Life

Hobbies

Irving is not just a basketball machine, and has many hobbies and personal endeavors. He often uploads comical videos to the video platform Vine, and he plays the saxophone and baritone. He has shown an interest in a variety of art forms, from music to acting and movie production. He also directed the third installment of the Uncle Drew series, which featured Nate Robinson and Maya Moore. The Uncle Drew series started out as a Pepsi advertisement where Kyrie dresses up as an old man to challenge and humiliate basketball players in local ballparks. Uncle Drew became one of Kyrie's NBA nicknames and he became one of the league's most popular players because of the ad.

Charity and Public Service Work

Irving has worked with UNICEF and done charity work in Africa, promoting education and sports as a means of bettering one's opportunities. He has also given back to his New Jersey roots by running fundraisers to help prevent St. Patrick's from closing down. The main causes he supports are health, human and children's rights, poverty, and slavery.

Uncle Drew Phenomenon

Pepsi's viral marketing campaign rocketed Irving to fame in the mainstream media. The ad, which showcased Irving's sense of humor, was a genius marketing tactic that showed businesses what an amazing advertisement looked like. Adam Harter, VP of Consumer Engagement, understands what the ad did for digital marketing:

> The success of 'Uncle Drew' changed the way all of us at Pepsi now think of digital marketing. It

comes at a time where advertising is going from the interruptive model of trying to get your attention while you are watching something that you want to watch, to a model that is more inviting, where people actually want to watch the engaging content that you produce.

From a basketball standpoint, the old man setup highlighted Irving's craftiness in the eyes of a mainstream audience. Irving crossing over and dunking as an old man with a beer belly in a playground setting captivated viewers. He said in an interview with the *Huffington Post*, "We all know that old guy that comes to the park, and either he's good or he's terrible."

The original video has attracted over 34 million views, and resulted in many trending topics and hashtags, like #UncleDrew and #DontReachYoungBlood. The success of the first ad campaign spurred the production of two more ads featuring future teammate Kevin Love in the second episode, and Nate Robinson in the third.

In these ads, fans got to see a different side of Irving that he doesn't get to showcase on the court. In high school interviews, he often mentioned how he is like most other kids, and has been reported during workout sessions to recite dialogue from the cartoon Spongebob Squarepants. He has always wanted people to know the side of him that just likes to have fun, and this was his chance.

Uncle Drew was an extension of the type of person that Kyrie Irving is. He is fun-loving, funny, wacky, confident, and very relaxed as a person. Kyrie's natural personality was what made the Uncle Drew phenomenon very successful and popular throughout the world.

Family

Kyrie Irving's father is Drederick Irving and his mother was the late Elizabeth Irving. Drederick was a professional basketball player playing in Australia when Kyrie was born. Drederick was the biggest influence on Kyrie's basketball career as he raised him almost singlehandedly on an NBA dream founded upon the game of basketball. He instilled the proper skills and values that Kyrie needed in order to become one of the best point guards in the world today. Kyrie's mother, Elizabeth, died when Kyrie was barely four years old. This led Drederick to raise Kyrie and the eldest daughter Asia all by himself. Drederick would later remarry a lady named Shetellia. Asia is a year older than Kyrie and she currently works as a model and finished with a degree in Accounting at Temple University. The youngest Irving is London. She was born to Drederick's second wife and Kyrie's step mother Shetellia.

Kyrie also has a daughter named Azurie Elizabeth who was born late November 2015.[ix] The mother of Kyrie's daughter is 2010 Miss Texas United States Andrea Wilson. The two started dating in 2013 but have since separated.[x]

Chapter 8: Irving's Legacy and Future

Irving has set a unique standard as a basketball player, separating himself from other NBA players by showing himself as a multifaceted talent on and off the court. He still has much to do if he wants to build a lasting legacy, but at his current pace, he is set to be a perennial all-star.

Kyrie's offensive skill set is almost exclusive to him even when compared to the many great point guards in today's NBA. As the NBA is now becoming a league dominated by point guards, Irving remains in the conversation as the best because of his transcendent offensive abilities. Kyrie Irving has arguably the best ball-handling ability in the NBA and can only be rivaled in that regard by Stephen Curry. When you talk about crossovers, nobody can contend with Irving's ability to trick defenders with the most popular dribble move. His crossovers and his ball handles are reminiscent of a great NBA guard named Allen Iverson. Iverson, despite barely being 6 feet tall, had all the tricks in the bag when it came to dribbling moves. His crossovers were the stuff of legends and he even crossed Michael Jordan once in his rookie year. Iverson became arguably the best pound-for-pound scorer in NBA history and he did a lot of it with his ball-handling ability.

Kyrie Irving worked on what Iverson brought to the league. While Kyrie, at nearly 6'3", is bigger a player compared to AI, Irving nonetheless needed the same type of dribbles that made Iverson famous to be able to contend with the best players in the NBA. Many of today's best players are point guards and most teams have point men playing at an elite level. With quick point guards guarding him, Kyrie needs every trick in the book to be able to elude athletic point guards such as Russell Westbrook, Erick Bledsoe, and Derrick Rose in order to put up numbers in the scoring column.

While most players with sick ball handles made a living on penetrating to the basket to score or dish out, Kyrie Irving can also hit jump shots at a very high level. He is not simply a one-dimensional, attack-the-basket type of a player because Kyrie has a range that stretches well beyond the three-point basket. When he can't attack the shot blocker or when the paint is packed with defenders, Irving would rather get the defender on his heels in order to get open pull-up jump shots out on the perimeter. He often pulls up from outside the three-point arc and has shown himself to be a very capable shooter from that distance. As proof of his three-point marksmanship, Kyrie once scored 55 points including 11 three-pointers. His 11 threes in a single game are the second most in NBA history, behind only the 12 three-point baskets made by Kobe Bryant.

Though his skill set is very similar to Allen Iverson, Kyrie does not have the same type of mentality that AI had and he idolizes Kobe more.[xi] Iverson always wanted to score first because that was his makeup as a player. Thus, he was never regarded as a true point guard and often played as an off guard. But Kyrie is a true point guard, even though he has all the skills to score as much as he wanted to. Irving often prefers to facilitate for his teammates rather than score for himself. His assist numbers may not be so gaudy but he never hogs the ball too much in order to get assists and would rather have the ball moving. Hence, Kyrie is an ideal player for teams that employ a lot of ball movement. Moreover, Kyrie works a lot harder on improving his game than Iverson ever did in his career. With Kyrie's skill set focused mainly on his fundamental abilities rather than his athleticism, we could expect Irving to be able to play the NBA game at a very high level even at an advanced age. There have been a lot of NBA guards who maintained an excellent level of play even in their late 30s. Such players include Kobe Bryant, Steve Nash, Jason Kidd, John Stockton, and Tony Parker. All those players made their living on their fundamental skills rather than their athletic ability and that made them perennial threats even as they aged. Kyrie's ability to handle the ball and his knack of shooting from range are both assets that could get him playing at an All-Star pace even as he slows down with age. If he can continue to play at that kind of a level, we can expect him to rack up more individual awards and career milestones in years to come. Who knows? He could even be good enough to become a Hall of Famer.

Furthermore, a case can already be made for an eventual Hall of Fame induction. When Pyonin was asked what Irving might amount to in the future, he had high praise for the young player.

> Without a doubt, Kyrie will be a Hall of Famer. When you think of players who were number one first-round picks and went on to win Rookie of the Year, players like Shaq, LeBron James, Tim Duncan, and others come to mind. That's what we're talking about when asked about

Kyrie. Every year, there's a first-round draft pick and there's an NBA Rookie of the Year, but only every couple of years is the NBA graced with a force, and that's Kyrie. When Kyrie and I trained together every day, I was his sensei and he was my pupil. That's how we structured our relationship. He's a very special student of the game, and his journey is just starting. I'd like to see more talent built around Kyrie so he can leverage the team to win championships.

This is a solid case for Irving. As a first-overall-pick-winning Rookie of the Year and as a multiple-time All-Star, Irving is surrounded by legends, and he has won numerous other awards that only strengthen his case. His most recent achievement, winning MVP at FIBA, puts him with the likes of Kevin Durant and Shaquille O'Neal, who were the last two American basketball players to receive the same accolade. His selections as an NBA All-Star at the age of 20 and his All-Star start at the age of 21, as mentioned above, make him akin to Magic Johnson, Kobe Bryant, and other greats who have become All-Star players at a very early age in their careers. Overall, Kyrie Irving's early successes as an individual bode well for his shot to become a Hall of Famer.

With Irving possibly manning the point guard position for the Cavs for several years to come, especially as he is locked in with a huge contract with Cleveland, Kyrie has a chance of being the best Cavaliers point guard in franchise history. That accolade unarguably belongs to Mark Price as of this writing. But if Irving continues to play with the Cavs and does so at a high level with All-Star selections to boot, he has all the makings of supplanting Mark Price for that spot. Irving also has the makings of being the best player in Cavaliers history. Obviously, that honor belongs to LeBron James and it's not even close. But Irving certainly has the chance of being in the argument with LeBron if could bring an NBA title and a few MVP awards with him to Cleveland.

Even at a very early stage in his career, Kyrie Irving can already be considered as a top five member when discussing about the best players in Cavaliers franchise history. Not too many great players have donned the uniform of the Cleveland Cavaliers and that helps the case of Irving. But the lack of good players in the franchise's history is not the sole reason for Irving to be considered as an all-time franchise great. At the age of 24, Kyrie Irving is already a three-time All-Star and is on pace for his fourth straight selection. He is also averaging 20 points per game and about 5 assists a night in his career to further cement his place as a franchise great.

However, the lack of success of his team early in his career might seem to damage his case as a Hall of Famer and as a Cavs franchise all-time great. Yet, it is rare to see players in Irving's position, coming in as a first pick, who could quickly turn around a franchise centered around three All-Stars who could possibly bring an NBA title in years to come. Team success cannot be accounted for until enough seasons are played out and Kyrie Irving has a chance of cancelling out his first three unsuccessful seasons by reaching the playoffs consistently for the rest of his playing career or even by winning at least one NBA title. Once it is all said and done and even if judged by today's standards, Kyrie Irving is a once-in-a-lifetime kind of talent who has become a pioneer for an NBA era ushered by elite point guards and has a chance of getting atop the pedestal as one of the best in NBA and Cavaliers history.

Final Word/About the Author

I was born and raised in Norwalk, Connecticut. Growing up, I could often be found spending many nights watching basketball, soccer, and football matches with my father in the family living room. I love sports and everything that sports can embody. I believe that sports are one of most genuine forms of competition, heart, and determination. I write my works to learn more about influential athletes in the hopes that from my writing, you the reader can walk away inspired to put in an equal if not greater amount of hard work and perseverance to pursue your goals. If you enjoyed *Kyrie Irving: The Inspiring Story of One of Basketball's Most Versatile Point Guards*, please leave a review! Also, you can read more of my works on *Michael Jordan, LeBron James, Klay Thompson, Stephen Curry, Kevin Durant, Russell Westbrook, Anthony Davis, Chris Paul, Blake Griffin, Kobe Bryant, Joakim Noah, Scottie Pippen, Carmelo*

Anthony, Kevin Love, Grant Hill, Tracy McGrady, Vince Carter, Patrick Ewing, Karl Malone, Tony Parker, Allen Iverson, Hakeem Olajuwon, Reggie Miller, Michael Carter-Williams, John Wall, James Harden, Tim Duncan, Steve Nash, LaMarcus Aldridge, Derrick Rose, Paul George, Kevin Garnett, J.J. Watt, Colin Kaepernick, Aaron Rodgers, Peyton Manning, Tom Brady, and Russell Wilson in the Kindle Store. If you love basketball, check out my website at claytongeoffreys.com to join my exclusive list where I let you know about my latest books and give you lots of goodies.

Like what you read?

If you love books on life, basketball, or productivity, check out my website at claytongeoffreys.com to join my exclusive list where I let you know about my latest books. Aside from being the first to hear about my latest releases, you can also download a free copy of *33 Life Lessons: Success Principles, Career Advice & Habits of Successful People.* See you there!

References

[i] Guardado, Maria. "How Kyrie Irving, a Kid from NJ, became LeBron James' Wingman on Cleveland Cavaliers". *New Jersey*. 16 April 2015. Web

[ii] "Kyrie Irving". *NBA Draft*. Web

[iii] "Kyrie Irving". *NBA Draft*. Web

[iv] "Kyrie Irving". *NBA Draft*. Web

[v] "Kyrie Irving". *NBA Draft*. Web

[vi] "Kyrie Irving". *NBA Draft*. Web

[vii] "Kyrie Irving". *Draft Express*. Web

[viii] Hidalgo, Vincent Paul. "Kobe Bryant Names Kyrie Irving And Russell Westbrook As Favourite Players". *International Business Times*. 15 March 2015. Web

[ix] Fedor, Chris. "Kyrie Irving announces birth of his daughter, says 'she came into the world to bring a shine to my world'". *Cleveland*. 24 November 2015. Web

[x] Connor, Star. "Kyrie Irving & Andrea Wilson Welcome Daughter, Azurie Elizabeth". *M Stars News*. 25 November 2015. Web

[xi] McMenamin Dave. "Cavs' Kyrie Irving: Game will never be the same without idol Kobe Bryant". *ESPN*. 3 December 2015

Made in the USA
Lexington, KY
15 February 2016